Barbara Jordan

CIVIL RIGHTS LEADER

by Connor Stratton

FOCUS READERS®

READERS®

BEACON

www.focusreaders.com

Focus Readers is distributed by North Star Editions: sales@northstareditions.com | 888-417-0195

Produced for Focus Readers by Red Line Editorial.

Photographs ©: Thomas J. O'Halloran/US News & World Report Magazine Photograph Collection/ Library of Congress, cover, 1; AP Images, 4, 6, 19, 20–21, 29; nsf/Alamy, 8; JWG/AP Images, 11; Shutterstock Images, 12, 17, 22, 27; Tom Colburn/Houston Chronicle/AP Images, 14; Dave Einsel/ Houston Chronicle/AP Images, 25

Library of Congress Cataloging-in-Publication Data
Names: Stratton, Connor, author.
Title: Barbara Jordan : civil rights leader / by Connor Stratton.
Description: Lake Elmo, MN : Focus Readers, [2021] | Series: Important
  Women | Includes index. | Audience: Grades 4-6
Identifiers: LCCN 2020033541 (print) | LCCN 2020033542 (ebook) | ISBN
  9781644936894 (hardcover) | ISBN 9781644937259 (paperback) | ISBN
  9781644937976 (pdf) | ISBN 9781644937617 (ebook)
Subjects: LCSH: Jordan, Barbara, 1936-1996--Juvenile literature. | United
  States. Congress. House--Biography--Juvenile literature. |
  Legislators--United States--Biography--Juvenile literature. | African
  American women legislators--Biography--Juvenile literature. | African
  American women legislators--Texas--Biography--Juvenile literature. |
  Texas--Politics and government--1951---Juvenile literature.
Classification: LCC E840.8.J62 S73 2021 (print) | LCC E840.8.J62 (ebook)
  | DDC 328.73/092 [B]--dc23
LC record available at https://lccn.loc.gov/2020033541
LC ebook record available at https://lccn.loc.gov/2020033542

Printed in the United States of America
Mankato, MN
012021

About the Author

Connor Stratton writes and edits children's books. He loves poetry and history, especially by and about fierce women. Every day he works to be a better feminist. He lives in Minnesota.

Table of Contents

Chapter 1

A Speech to Impeach

On July 25, 1974, millions of people watched Barbara Jordan on TV. She was giving an important speech. **Congress** had a tough decision to make. President Richard Nixon had acted wrongly.

Barbara Jordan was part of the House Judiciary Committee, a group that focuses on justice in government.

Mr. EILBERG

▷ Jordan studies the US Constitution during the debate about impeachment.

Congress could vote to **impeach** him. It could also remove him from office. But many lawmakers were not sure what to do.

The US **Constitution** gave Congress only certain powers.

Some people thought impeaching Nixon was not the right use of those powers.

Jordan's speech helped many people decide. She described why Nixon's actions were wrong. She explained why he should leave office.

Did You Know?

Nixon believed Congress would remove him from office. So, he resigned. He left office in August 1974.

Chapter 2

Early Life

Barbara Jordan was born on February 21, 1936. She grew up in Houston, Texas. She had two sisters. The family lived in an all-Black neighborhood. White lawmakers had segregated the city.

 Jordan grew up in a part of Houston known as the Fifth Ward.

Laws forced Black people to live in areas where white people did not.

Barbara loved public speaking. In high school, she won speaking contests. She led her college debate team, too. The team beat colleges across the country. It even tied with Harvard, one of the top schools in the world.

Jordan learned to give great speeches. She found important facts. And she planned out her ideas. Jordan knew that lawyers

In 1977, Harvard gave Jordan (waving) an honorary law degree.

needed these skills. So, in 1956, she started law school. She moved to Boston, Massachusetts.

The Texas State Senate meets in a room inside the state's capitol building.

Jordan earned her law degree three years later. Then she moved back to Houston. She worked as a lawyer there.

She became interested in politics, too. In 1960, Jordan helped with John F. Kennedy's run for president.

Then she ran for office herself.
Jordan ran for the Texas House
twice. She lost both times. But in
1966, she ran for the Texas State
Senate. This time, she won.

Jordan became Texas's first Black
state senator in 83 years. And she
was Texas's first Black female state
senator ever.

Did You Know?

Jordan's great-grandfather was one of
Texas's first Black lawmakers.

Chapter 3

Making Change

Being a Black woman in the Texas Senate was not easy. All the other lawmakers were white men. Many of them were **racist**. Many were **sexist**, too. But Jordan believed she could still make changes.

 As a lawmaker, Jordan worked to protect people who faced discrimination or unfair treatment.

She learned how the Texas Senate worked. She became friends with the lawmakers. Jordan got them to support her plans. She helped pass the state's first minimum wage law. It said companies could not pay workers less than a certain amount. Jordan also helped get more money for people who were hurt at work. In addition, she helped end several segregation laws.

In 1972, Jordan won a seat in the US House of Representatives.

 The House of Representatives is one of the two chambers of the US Congress.

She had a huge success in 1975. The Voting Rights Act was about to end. This law made sure that Black people could vote. Jordan worked hard to keep the law. She wrote parts of a new Voting Rights Act.

She also got lawmakers to vote for the new law.

The new Voting Rights Act passed. It continued protecting Black Americans. It helped other groups, too. The law made sure Mexican Americans could vote. It also helped Asian Americans and American Indians.

Did You Know?

Jordan was the first woman to give the main speech at the Democratic National Convention.

> **Jordan greets the crowd during her famous speech at the Democratic National Convention in 1976.**

Some people said Jordan's laws did not do enough. Jordan often agreed. She wanted stronger laws as well. But she believed that some change was better than none.

The Voting Rights Act

Racism has a long history in the United States. White people enslaved Black people for nearly 250 years. Slavery ended after the Civil War (1861–1865). But many white people still wanted power. They passed laws that stopped Black people from voting.

In the 1950s, the **civil rights movement** led to new laws. One was the Voting Rights Act of 1965. It said states must let Black people vote. The law brought huge changes. Many more Black people voted. They elected leaders who shared their values.

Hundreds of people vote in Alabama in 1966.

Chapter 4

After Congress

Jordan left Congress in 1979. She didn't want to hold office anymore. And she had a serious disease. She took a job at a college. She didn't have to travel as much. That made it easier to deal with her health.

 Jordan taught at the Lyndon B. Johnson School of Public Affairs in Texas.

Jordan taught politics. She helped her students think and learn. She even helped them after they finished school. Her students often got jobs working in government.

Jordan kept giving speeches around the country. She also stayed active in politics. For example,

 Jordan spoke at the Democratic National Convention for the second time in 1992.

she started helping the United Nations in 1985. She worked against **apartheid** in South Africa. In the 1990s, she helped the US government make decisions about **immigration**.

Jordan died in 1996. But her work continued to make a difference. For instance, the 1975 Voting Rights Act helped more people of color get elected. Between 1970 and 1985, the number of Latino people elected nearly tripled. And by 2020, that number had doubled again.

Did You Know?

In 1994, President Bill Clinton gave Jordan the Presidential Medal of Freedom. It is one of the top US honors.

A statue at the University of Texas at Austin honors Jordan and her work.

During her career, Jordan had jobs that few other Black women held. She showed Black women and girls their power. In fact, she showed the whole country.

FOCUS ON
Barbara Jordan

Write your answers on a separate piece of paper.

1. Write a sentence summarizing the main ideas of Chapter 4.

2. If you ran for office, which issues would be most important to you? Why?

3. When was Barbara Jordan elected to the US House of Representatives?
   - A. 1966
   - B. 1972
   - C. 1996

4. How did Barbara Jordan show Black women and girls their power?
   - A. Jordan was the first Black woman in many different positions of power.
   - B. Jordan's laws only helped Black women and girls.
   - C. Jordan taught only Black female students.

5. What does **politics** mean in this book?

*She became interested in **politics**, too. In 1960, Jordan helped with John F. Kennedy's run for president.*

    A. teaching at a college
    B. running long distances
    C. activities related to government

6. What does **segregated** mean in this book?

*White lawmakers had **segregated** the city. Laws forced Black people to live in areas where white people did not.*

    A. separated groups of people based on race
    B. bought homes for certain people to live in
    C. passed laws that fought against racism

Answer key on page 32.

Glossary

apartheid
A system of racial segregation in South Africa from the late 1940s until the 1990s.

civil rights movement
A mass struggle against racial discrimination in the United States in the 1950s and 1960s.

Congress
The group of people who make laws for the United States.

Constitution
The document that lays out the basic beliefs and laws of the United States.

immigration
The process of moving to a new country to live permanently.

impeach
To bring formal charges against someone serving in office to determine if that person is guilty of a crime.

racist
Having to do with hatred or mistreatment of people because of their skin color or ethnicity.

sexist
Having to do with hatred or mistreatment of people because of their gender.

To Learn More

BOOKS

Anderson, Jennifer Joline. *Exploring Voting and Elections.* Minneapolis: Lerner Publications, 2020.

Barton, Chris. *What Do You Do with a Voice Like That? The Story of Extraordinary Congresswoman Barbara Jordan.* New York: Beach Lane Books, 2018.

Harris, Duchess, and Deirdre R. J. Head. *Barbara Jordan: Politician and Civil Rights Leader.* Minneapolis: Abdo Publishing, 2019.

NOTE TO EDUCATORS

Visit **www.focusreaders.com** to find lesson plans, activities, links, and other resources related to this title.

Index

C
civil rights movement, 20
Congress, 5–7, 23

E
Earl, Nancy, 24

H
Houston, Texas, 9, 12

L
lawmakers, 6, 9, 13,
    15–16, 18
lawyer, 11–12

N
Nixon, Richard, 5–7

S
segregation, 9, 16

T
Texas State Senate, 13,
    15–16

U
US Constitution, 6
US House of
    Representatives, 16

V
Voting Rights Act, 17–18,
    20, 26

Answer Key: 1. Answers will vary; **2.** Answers will vary; **3.** B; **4.** A; **5.** C; **6.** A